Victoria Fromkin
Robert Rodman

AN
INTRODUCTION TO LANGUAGE
Fifth Edition

Answers to Exercises

Karen Wallace
UCLA

The camera-ready manuscript for this booklet was prepared with emTeX, a PC version of the LaTeX document preparation system. LaTeX was developed by Leslie Lamport to augment the TeX document prepration system, created by Donald Knuth. EmTeX was written by Eberhard Mattes and is free software. Texcad, the drawing program used, was written by Georg Horn and is shareware. The phonetics fonts used here were developed by Emma Pease.

ISBN: 0-03-054984-1

Address Editorial Correspondence To: Harcourt Brace Jovanovich, Inc.
301 Commerce Street, Suite 3700
Fort Worth, Texas 76102

Address Orders To: Harcourt Brace Jovanovich, Inc.
6277 Sea Harbor Drive
Orlando, Florida 32887
1-800-782-4479, or 1-800-433-0001 (in Florida)

Printed in the United States of America.

6 7 8 9 0 1 2   0 2 3   9 8 7 6 5 4

Contents

Chapter 1

Language

1. *Sound sequences.* Any word which conforms to the sound pattern of English is a correct answer. Existing English words as names of new products are also acceptable; for example, *Kleen* or *Clean* as the name of a laundry soap.

2. *Judgments.* Some judgments may vary across dialects.

   a. **Robin forced the sheriff go.*
      The word *to* is missing in front of the verb *go*. The verb *force* requires a *to* infinitival in the embedded clause.

   f. **He came a large sum of money by.*
      Some (but not all) verb–particle pairs (such as *put away* or *look up* can be split, with the particle going to the right of the direct object. *Pass by* can be split in this way, but *come by* is one of the verb–particle pairs that cannot be split.

   g. **Did in a corner little Jack Horner sit?*
      A yes–no question must start with an auxiliary verb, like *did*; but the element following the auxiliary verb must be the subject of the sentence. Here, the second element is the prepositional phrase *in a corner*.

   h. **Elizabeth is resembled by Charles.*
      The verb *resemble* does not occur in passive sentences.

   k. **It is eager to love a kitten.*
      If the word *it* refers to an animate (but nonhuman) thing (e.g., a dog), the sentence is grammatical. If the word *it* is the nonreferential expletive, the sentence is ungrammatical because the adjective *eager* must have a referential subject.

1

l. *That birds can fly amazes.*

Amaze is a transitive verb; it requires a direct object. Compare *That birds can fly amazes Fred.*

n. *Has the nurse slept the baby yet?*

The verb *sleep* is intransitive; it cannot take a direct object.

o. *I was surprised for you to get married.*

The adjective *surprised* requires a tensed sentential complement (i.e., *that you got married*) and cannot take an infinitival one.

p. *I wonder who and Mary went swimming.*

The verb *wonder* requires a WH-phrase in the complementizer position of the embedded clause. *Who* is a WH-phrase; *I wonder who went swimming* is grammatical. *Who and Mary* is not a WH-phrase.

q. *Myself bit John.*

Reflexive noun phrases like *myself* need a coreferent antecedent (another NP which refers to the same person or object) in the same clause. There is no antecedent for *myself* in this sentence.

3. *Onomatopoeic words.* Sample answers are given below.

   (a) suush — what you do when you ski
   (b) thock — the sound of a baseball hitting a mitt
   (c) zoop — what a zipper does
   (d) grach — what a rusty door hinge does
   (e) glup — swallow
   (f) gollum — swallow (taken from the name of a character in J.R.R. Tolkien's *The Hobbit*)

4. *Non-arbitrary and arbitrary signs.* Sample answers are given below.

   (a) Non-arbitrary signs:
   - signs at international airports (e.g., a picture of a knife and fork indicating a restaurant)
   - the wheelchair sign which indicates parking is for disabled only
   - circle and slash signs (e.g., "no smoking")
   - some signs made by a referee at a football game
   - a fuel indicator with a picture of a tank

   (b) Arbitrary signs:
   - a signal from a coach to a baseball player at bat

- significant clothing (e.g., a black armband for someone in mourning)
- the U.S. zip code system
- a fuel indicator that reads E ... F

5. *Learning.* The first statement is quite probable. The second statement is not very likely, since most sentences are not learned or memorized, but rather constructed freely. Some sentences, such as slogans or sentences from a foreign language, may be learned as a whole.

6. *Human and animal communication.*

   Similarities. Animal sounds and human language share physical characteristics: both are transmitted by sound waves produced in the vocal tract with lung air. Some imitative bird sounds resemble human speech. Both are systems of communication.

   Differences. Animal communication is invariant; human language is infinitely creative in the kinds of messages transmitted. Animal messages cannot be segmented into independently meaningful parts, the way sentences of all human languages can be. Animal messages are stimulus-controlled, while human messages are more than a simple response to stimuli.

7. *Communication system of a wolf.* No. The system the wolf uses is finite (though large) and restricted to a limited set of messages, while human language is capable of expressing an infinite number of unrestricted messages. A wolf is unable to produce new messages using a different combination of independently meaningful gestures.

8. *A dog's understanding of speech.* No. Even if the dog learned to respond to the given cues in the correct way, it would not be learning language since its response is driven solely by those cues—it is stimulus-controlled behavior. There is no creative aspect to the system; the dog could not associate a novel combination of cues with a complex action.

9. *"Correct" rules of grammar.* Here is a sample answer: one is often taught in English classes that it is incorrect to end a sentence with a preposition, yet *"What are you putting those marbles into?"* is more natural for the majority of English speakers (including teachers of English) than *"Into what are you putting those marbles?"*

Chapter 2

Morphology

1. *English morphemes.*

   (a) retro + act + ive

   (b) be + friend + ed

   (c) tele + vise

   (d) margin

   (e) en + dear + ment

   (f) psycho + logy

   (g) un + palat + able

   (h) holi + day

   (i) grand + mother

   (j) morph + em + ic

2. *Zulu morphology.*

   A. Zulu nouns

      a. um-

      b. aba-

      c.

Zulu	English
fazi	'married woman'
fana	'boy'
zali	'parent'
fundisi	'teacher'
bazi	'carver'
limi	'farmer'
dlali	'player'
fundi	'reader'

B. Zulu verbs

    d. -a

    e. -i

    f. A noun is formed by adding the suffix *-i* to the stem (and adding a singular or plural prefix). Schematically,

       Noun = Stem + i

    g. fund

    h. baz

3. *Identify morphological sequences.*

    (a) 3.

    (b) 7.

    (c) 1.

    (d) 6.

    (e) 5.

    (f) 4.

4. *Identify morphological elements.*

    (a) 3.

    (b) 1.

    (c) 4.

    (d) 2.

5. *Dutch morphology.*

    (a) To form an infinitive in Dutch, suffix *-en* to the root. Schematically,
Infinitive = root + *en*

    (b) To form a past participle in Dutch, circumfix *ge* + *d* to the root. Schematically,
Past Participle = *ge* + root + *d*

6. *Japanese verb forms.* Note that this is only one of a number of possible solutions.

(a)

Gloss	Basic Verb Stem	Gloss	Basic Verb Stem
call	yob	leave	de
write	kak	go out	dekake
eat	tabe	read	yom
see	mi	die	shin
lend	kas	close	shime
wait	mat	wear	ki

(b) Add the suffix *–ru* if the stem ends in a vowel, and *–u* otherwise.

Note that students might hypothesize that the *r* in words like *miru* "see" is part of the stem. This would make the rule above somewhat simpler: it would be something like "suffix *–u* to the verb stem." However, it would complicate the rule to be written in part (c).

(c) Add the suffix *–masu* if the verb stem ends in a vowel, and *–imasu* otherwise.

(d) To derive the formal forms from the informal forms, (1) if the informal form ends in *–ru*, replace *–ru* with *–masu*; (2) if the informal form ends in *–u*, replace *–u* with *–imasu*. Note: rules (1) and (2) are disjunctively ordered.

7. *Swahili.*

(a)

–toto	child
–fika	arrive
m–	noun prefix attached to singular Class I nouns
wa–	noun prefix attached to plural Class I nouns
a–	prefix attached to verbs when subject is a singular Class I noun
wa–	prefix attached to verbs when subject is a plural Class I noun
me–	prefix attached to verbs to indicate past tense
na–	prefix attached to verbs to indicate present progressive tense
ta–	prefix attached to verbs to indicate future tense
–tu	man
–lala	sleep
–su	knife
–anguka	fall
ki–	noun prefix attached to singular nouns of Class II
vi–	noun prefix attached to plural nouns of Class II
ki–	prefix attached to verbs when subject is a singular Class II noun
vi–	prefix attached to verbs when subject is a plural Class II noun
–kapu	basket

7

(b) The verb is constructed by stringing together, in order from left to right, (1) the verbal prefix indicating the noun class, (2) the verbal prefix indicating the tense, and (3) the verbal stem. Schematically,

Verb = Class Prefix + Tense prefix + Stem

(c) (1) mtoto anaanguka
    (2) vikapu vimefika
    (3) mtu ataanguka

8. *Reduplication in Samoan.*

   (a) (1) lalaga
       (2) savavali
       (3) pese

   (b) To form a plural verb form, reduplicate (copy) the penultimate (next to last) CV syllable. Stated another way: to form a plural verb form, insert a copy of the penultimate syllable before (or after) that syllable.

   Here is the same rule, stated more formally:

   $[+V, +\text{plural}]: \ /XC_1V_1C_2V_2/ \rightarrow /XC_1V_1C_1V_1C_2V_2/,$

   where X is any sequence of C and V (or null).

9. *Incorrect definitions.* The following are sample answers.

   (a) *stalemate, "husband or wife no longer interested"*
       The definition results from incorrectly interpreting this word as a compound of *stale* and *mate* and putting the meanings of those words together, where *stale* means 'flat, tasteless' and *mate* is 'husband or wife'.

   (b) *effusive, "able to be merged"*
       This word looks like it is formed from the stem *fuse*, meaning 'merge'; the prefix *e*, which means 'out' or 'from', as in *eradicate*; and the suffix -*ive* 'able to be'.

   (c) *tenet, "a group of ten singers"*
       This word has been interpreted as a combination of *ten* and the -*et* of words like *quartet* and *octet*.

(d) *dermatology, "a study of derms"*

Here, the student has recognized the *–(o)logy* of words like *biology, philology* and generalized its meaning, even though he/she probably had no idea what a *derm* might be!

(e) *ingenious, "not very smart"*

This word was misanalyzed as a combination of the *in–* of words like *incompetent* (which means 'not') and the word *genius*. But notice that *in–* doesn't generally attach to nouns.

(f) *finesse, "a female fish"*

The word was interpreted as the noun *fin* 'fish appendage', plus the suffix *–ess* 'female' from words like *lioness*.

10. *Acronyms.* The following are sample answers:

(a) UPS: United Parcel Service

ASCII: American Standard Code for Information Interchange (used with computers)

ROM: Read Only Memory (computer memory)

OPEC: Organization of Petroleum Exporting Countries

NASA: National Aeronautics and Space Administration

DOA: dead on arrival

AKA: also known as

TLC: tender loving care

IMHO: in my humble opinion

OBO: or best offer (from classified ads)

(b) WORM — World Organization for the Raising of Mollusks

ATB — around the bend

TIOLI — take it or leave it

PATUI — People Against The Use of Invective

(etc.)

Chapter 3

Syntax

1. *Linguistic knowledge.* Sample answers:

   (a) *Structural ambiguity.*

   Example: *We filled the room with the boxes.*

   This sentence is structurally ambiguous. The phrase *with the boxes* can modify the noun *room* (with the meaning that we crowded into the room that had the boxes in it), or it can modify the verb *fill* (with the meaning that we put a lot of boxes in the room).

   (b) *Paraphrases.*

   Example: *Susie is studying algebra.*
                   What Susie is studying is algebra.

   These two sentences have the same meaning but different structures; they are paraphrases of each other.

   (c) *Meaning relations.*

   Example: *This problem is difficult for me to solve.*

   The NP *this problem* is logically (and semantically) the direct object of the verb *solve*, although structurally it is the subject of the sentence.

2. *The recursive nature of language.*

   A. A possible answer would be: (d) We know that he knows that you know that I hate war.

   B. These sentences show that there is no "longest" sentence in English; one can go on indefinitely, constructing longer and longer sentences by appending "He/she knows that" to the previously constructed sentence. This illustrates the recursive nature of the phrase structure rules that characterize sentences and verb phrases.

C. While it is true that in principle we could construct a sentence of indefinite length (a fact about linguistic *competence*), in actual behavior there are lapses of memory and mistakes, and we would eventually have to stop constructing a longer sentence in order to eat, drink, and sleep. These are facts about linguistic *performance*.

3. *Disambiguation with paraphrases.*

(a) *Dick finally decided on the boat.*

    i. Dick finally chose the boat.

    ii. Dick made the decision when he was on the boat.

(b) *The professor's appointment was shocking.*

    i. It was shocking that the professor was appointed.

    ii. The appointment made by the professor was shocking.

(c) *The design has big squares and circles.*

    i. The squares and circles in the design are big.

    ii. There are circles and big squares in the design.

(d) *That sheepdog is too hairy to eat.*

    i. That sheepdog can't eat because he is so hairy.

    ii. No one could eat such a hairy sheepdog.

(e) *Could this be the invisible man's hair tonic?*

    i. Could this be the hair tonic belonging to the invisible man?

    ii. Could this be the invisible hair tonic for men?

(f) *The governor is a dirty street fighter.*

    i. The governor fights against dirty streets.

    ii. The governor fights unfairly in the streets.

    iii. The governor is a dirty individual who fights in the street.

(g) *I cannot recommend him too highly.*

    i. He is superb; nothing I can say would exaggerate his abilities.

    ii. He is mediocre; I cannot recommend him very highly.

(h) *Terry loves his wife and so do I.*

    i. Terry loves his wife and I love Terry's wife too.

    ii. Terry loves his wife and I love my wife.

(i) *They said she would go yesterday.*

    i. Yesterday they said "She will go."

    ii. They said that yesterday was the day she would go.

(j) *How much do you want to cut the grass?*

    i. How much money do you want for cutting the grass?

    ii. How eager are you to cut the grass?

4. *Representing structural ambiguity.*

The magician touched the child with the wand.

Meaning 1: The magician used a wand to touch the child.

Tree 1:

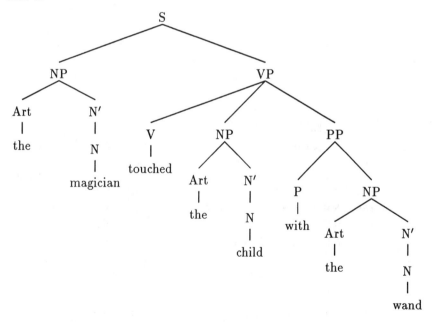

Meaning 2 : The magician touched the child that had a wand.

Tree 2:

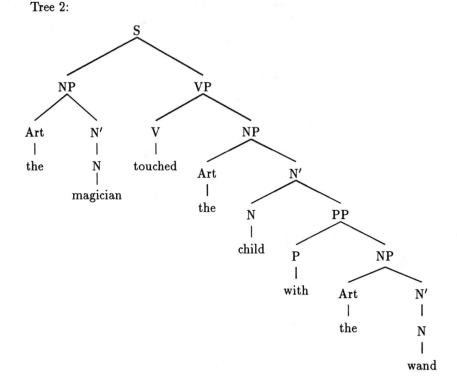

5. *Phrase structure rule expansions.*

(a)	S′ → Comp S	(j)	NP → Art N
(b)	S′ → S	(k)	NP → Pronoun
(c)	S → NP Aux VP	(l)	VP → V NP PP
(d)	S → NP VP	(m)	VP → V NP
(e)	NP → Art Adj Adj N PP	(n)	VP → V PP
(f)	NP → Art Adj Adj N	(o)	VP → V
(g)	NP → Art Adj N PP	(p)	VP → V S′
(h)	NP → Art Adj N	(q)	PP → P NP
(i)	NP → Art N PP		

6. *Embedded sentences.* Below, italics represent underlining.

   (a) Yesterday I noticed *my accountant repairing the toilet and my plumber computing my taxes.*

   (b) Becky said that *Jake would play the piano.*

(c) I deplore the fact that *bats have wings*.

(d) That *Guinevere loves Lorian* is known to all my friends.

(e) Who promised the teacher that *Maxine wouldn't be absent*?

(f) It's ridiculous that *he washes his own Rolls-Royce*.

(g) The woman asked for *the waiter to bring a glass of ice water*.

(h) The person *who answers this question* will win $100.

(i) The idea of *Romeo marrying a 13-year-old* is upsetting.

(j) I gave my hat to the nurse *who helped me cut my hair*.

(k) For *your children to spend all your royalty payments on recreational drugs* is a shame.

(l) Give this fork to the person *I'm getting the pie for*.

(m) Khăw chŷa wăa *khruu maa*.

(n) Je me demande quand *il partira*.

(o) Jan zei dat *Piet dit boek niet heeft gelezen*.

7. *Phrase structure trees.*

   (a) The puppy found the child.

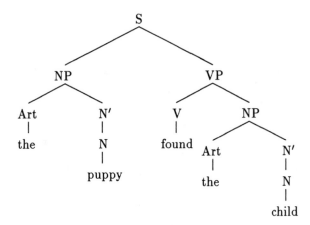

15

(b) A very frightened passenger landed the crippled airplane.

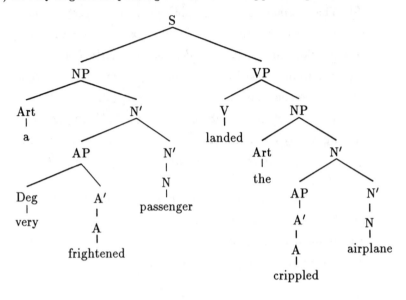

(c) The house on the hill collapsed in the wind.

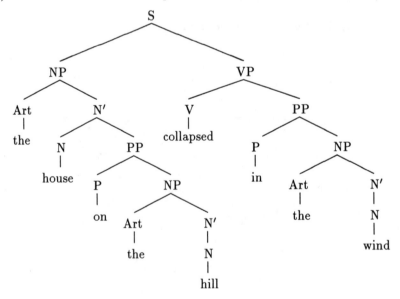

(d) The ice melted.

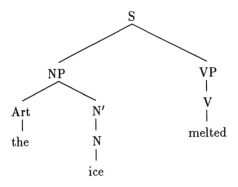

(e) The hot sun melted the ice.

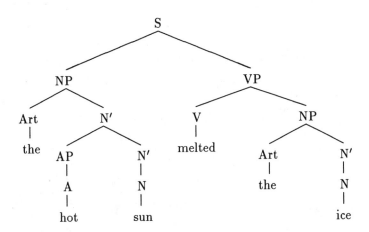

(f) A quaint old ivy-covered house appeared.

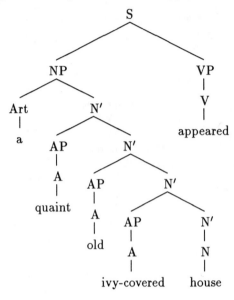

(g) The old tree swayed in the wind.

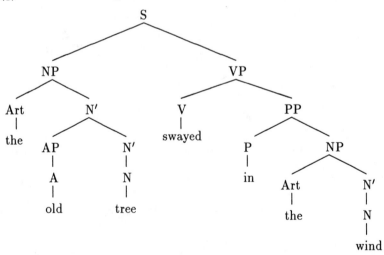

(h) The children put the toy in the box.

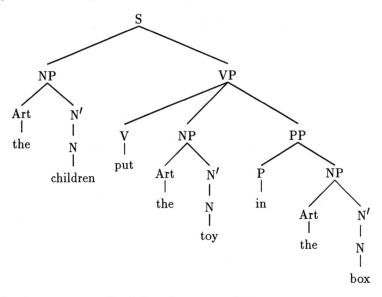

(i) The reporter realized that the senator lied.

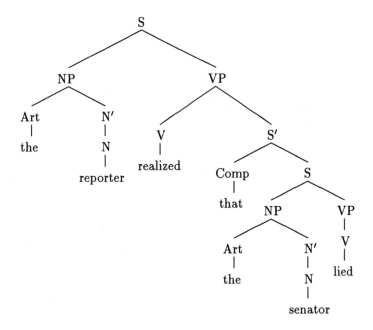

8. *Trees for sentences 6-10 words long.* Here are sample answers.

(a) The warship sank into the ocean. (6 words)

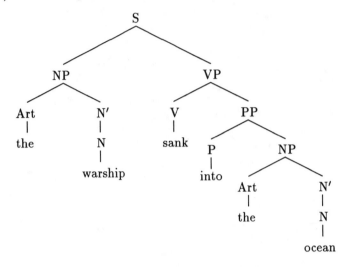

(b) The monkeys know that the bananas fall. (7 words)

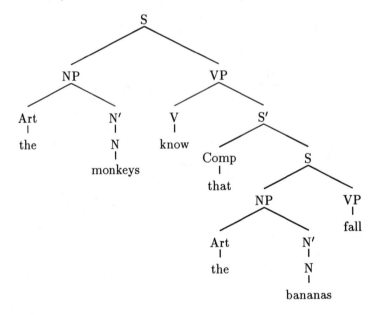

(c) The young kids with this strange allergy hiccup. (8 words)

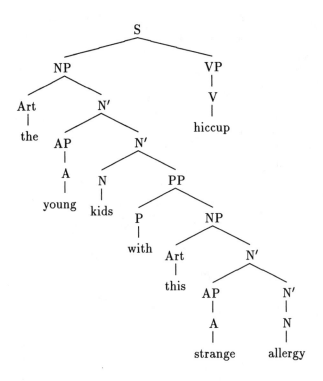

(d) An otter played in the mud on the bank. (9 words)

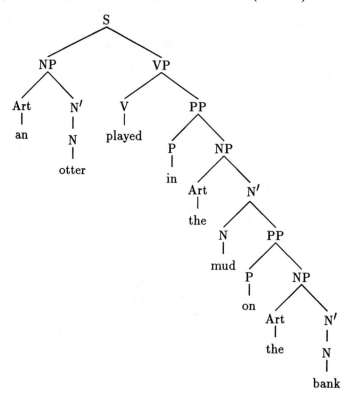

(e) The sleuth found a very old picture of the castle. (10 words)

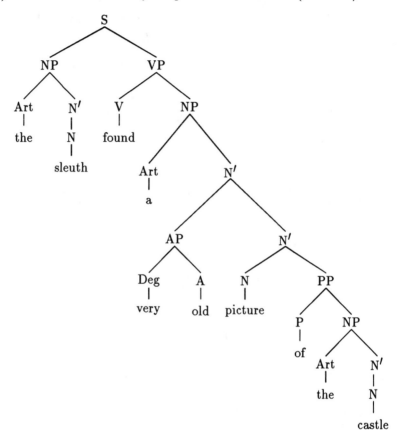

9. *All and only the grammatical sentences.* A grammar that generated all of the grammatical sentences plus a few that are not grammatical would not accurately characterize the syntactic knowledge that the speaker of the language has, because it would not be able to make distinctions between grammatical and ungrammatical sentences. Since the speaker of the language is able to make such distinctions, this is part of the speaker's knowledge; the grammar in question does not characterize that knowledge.

10. *Made-up phrase structure rules.*

(a) Here are three sample trees generated by these rules; there are an
infinite number of possible answers.

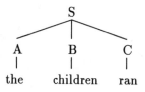

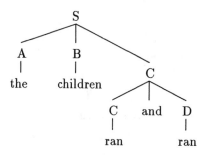

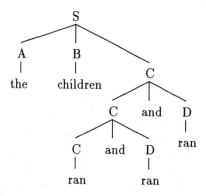

(b) These rules characterize an infinite number of constituent structure
trees, because rules (v) and (vi) are recursive.

11. *Recursion.*

(a) Noun Phrase recursion: sample answer

i. The boy in the house on the corner sneezed.
ii. The boy in the house on the corner of the street sneezed.

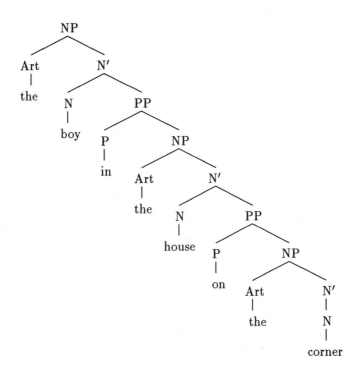

(b) Verb Phrase recursion: sample answer

    i. You know that she read the book.

    ii. We believe that you know that she read the book.

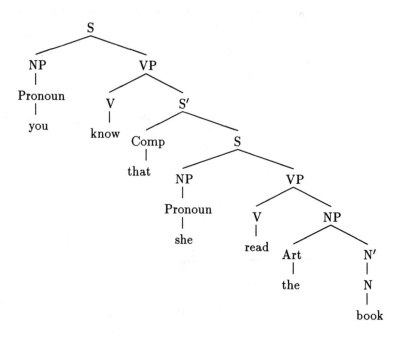

(c) Sentence recursion: sample answer

The same examples can be used here as in (b), since VP recursion and S recursion are both illustrated in (b).

12. *Phrasal Heads.*

	Phrase (NP or VP)	Head
a.	the puppy	puppy
	found the child	found
	the child	child
b.	a very frightened passenger	passenger
	landed the crippled airplane	landed
	the crippled airplane	airplane
c.	the house on the hill	house
	the hill	hill
	collapsed in the wind	collapsed
	the wind	wind
d.	the ice	ice
	melted	melted
e.	the hot sun	sun
	melted the ice	melted
	the ice	ice
f.	a quaint old ivy-covered house	house
	appeared	appeared
g.	the old tree	tree
	swayed in the wind	swayed
	the wind	wind
h.	the children	children
	put the toy in the box	put
	the toy	toy
	the box	box
i.	the reporter	reporter
	realized that the senator lied	realized
	the senator	senator
	lied	lied

13. *Subcategorization.*

   (a) **The man located.* The verb *locate* is transitive: it requires an NP object.

   <u>locate</u>: Verb, [__ NP]

   (b) **Jesus wept the apostles.* The verb *weep* is intransitive: it does not allow an object.

   <u>weep</u>: Verb, [__]

   (c) **Robert is hopeful of his children.* The adjective *hopeful* allows an S′ complement (*that his children will succeed* or no complement, but it cannot take a PP complement with *of*.

   <u>hopeful</u>: Adjective, [__ (S′)]

(d) *Robert is fond that his children love animals.* The adjective *fond* does subcategorize for a PP complement with *of*, and does not allow an S′ complement.

fond: Adjective, [__ PP[of]]

(e) *The children laughed the man.* Like *weep*, the verb *laugh* is intransitive and may not take a direct object; however, unlike *weep*, *laugh* allows a PP with *at*.

laugh: Verb, [__ (PP[at])]

14. *Ditransitive verbs.* Sample answers:

(a) bring: *The vassal brought the emperor a gift.*

(b) throw: *The pitcher threw Sam the ball.*

(c) call: *The activist called the senator a liar.*

Subcategorization for *call*:

call, V, [__ NP NP]

15. *Verb Classes.* Sample answers:

(a) like (*The group would like (for) Holly to sing.*)

(b) convince (*Molly convinced Max to open the door.*)

(c) start (*Kathryn started to pitch the tent.*)

(d) expect (*Shelley expected the meeting to be a waste of time.*)

(e) think (*Vic thought (that) she liked buildings.*)

16. *Long-distance correlations.* Sample answers:

(a) i. What do you think will compensate for the loss of Humboldt?
     ii. You think what will compensate for the loss of Humboldt?

(b) i. Which color has Percy decided on?
     ii. Percy has decided on which color?

(c) i. Where is Marcy going for her vacation?
     ii. Marcy is going where for her vacation?

17. *Systematic relationships: ditransitive verbs.* Each of these sentences has both a direct object — the NP acted upon, or Theme; and an indirect object — the recipient, or Goal, of the action. In the first sentence in each pair, the Goal NP immediately follows the verb, and is followed by the Theme NP; in the second sentence, the Theme NP immediately follows the verb, and is followed by a PP containing the Goal NP.

18. *Inter-language syntactic differences.* The following are sample answers.

  (a) *French:*

      i. French marks future tense on the main verb, while English marks future tense with an "auxiliary" verb.

      ii. In French, an adjective follows the noun it modifies, while in English an adjective precedes the noun it modifies.

      iii. In French, the adjective agrees in number and gender with the noun it modifies, while in English it does not.

      French is an SVO language.

  (b) *Japanese:*

      i. Japanese has subject markers and object markers which indicate grammatical relations in all noun phrases, while English does not.

      ii. In Japanese, the verb follows the object, while in English the object follows the verb.

      iii. In Japanese, the auxiliary *iru* follows the main verb, while in English auxiliaries always precede the main verb.

      Japanese is an SOV language.

  (c) *Swahili:*

      i. Swahili has *class markers*. These are prefixes that distinguish various classes of nouns and whether they are singular or plural. English has only plural suffixes.

      ii. Swahili verbs are marked for present and past tense with a prefix; English verbs are marked for tense with a suffix or with auxiliary verbs.

      iii. Swahili verbs also have prefixes agreeing in class and number with the subject, while English has nothing like this.

      Swahili is an SVO language.

  (d) *Korean:*

      i. Korean (like Japanese) has suffixes on all noun phrases indicating grammatical relations like subject and direct object, while in English the distinction only surfaces in pronouns.

      ii. Korean has verb suffixes which indicate whether the sentence is an assertion or a question. English has no such suffixes.

      iii. In a WH-question in Korean, the WH phrase does not necessarily occur at the beginning of the sentence, while in English it is always at the beginning.

Korean is an SOV language.

(e) *Tagalog:*

   i. In Tagalog proper names like *Pedro* occur with articles, while in English, they cannot.

   ii. In Tagalog the verb precedes the subject, while in English the subject precedes the verb.

   iii. In Tagalog there is are *topic markers*, while in English topics are not marked overtly.

Tagalog is a VSO language.

Chapter 4

Semantics

1. *Semantic properties.*

A. (a) bachelor, man, son, paperboy, pope, chief

   (b) bull, rooster, drake, ram

   The (a) and (b) words are **male animals**; the (a) words are **human**; the (b) words are **nonhuman**.

B. (a) table, stone, pencil, cup, house, ship, car

   (b) milk, alcohol, rice, soup, mud

   The (a) and (b) words are **concrete objects**; the (a) words are **countable** (count nouns); the (b) words are **uncountable** (mass nouns).

C. (a) book, temple, mountain, road, tractor

   (b) idea, love, charity, sincerity, bravery, fear

   The (a) and (b) words are **inanimate things**; the (a) words are **concrete**; the (b) words are **abstract**.

D. (a) pine, elm, ash, weeping willow, sycamore

   (b) rose, dandelion, aster, tulip, daisy

   The (a) and (b) words are **plants**; the (a) words are **trees**; the (b) words are **flowers**.

E. (a) book, letter, encyclopedia, novel, notebook, dictionary

(b) typewriter, pencil, ballpoint, crayon, quill, charcoal, chalk

The (a) and (b) words are **related to writing**; the (a) words are **things written**; the (b) words are **things to write with**.

F. (a) walk, run, skip, jump, hop, swim

(b) fly, skate, ski, ride, cycle, canoe, hang-glide

The (a) and (b) words are **motion verbs**; the (a) words are **motion without a vehicle**; the (b) words are **motion with a vehicle**.

G. (a) ask, tell, say, talk, converse

(b) shout, whisper, mutter, drawl, holler

The (a) and (b) words are **verbs of speaking**; the (a) words **do not indicate manner of speaking**; the (b) words **indicate manner of speaking**.

H. (a) alive, asleep, dead, married, pregnant

(b) tall, smart, interesting, bad, tired

The (a) and (b) words are **state of being adjectives**; the (a) words have **complementary** correlates (e.g., *alive–dead, asleep–awake*; the (b) words have **gradable** correlates (e.g., *tall–short, smart–stupid*).

I. (a) alleged, counterfeit, false, putative, accused

(b) red, large, cheerful, pretty, stupid

The (a) and (b) words are **descriptive adjectives**; the (a) words are **nonimplicational**: an *alleged* murderer is not necessarily a murderer; the (b) words are **implicational**: a *tall* murderer is necessarily a murderer. Note: the term *implicational* is not standard for this distinction. It is important only to understand what the distinction is.

2. *Semantic Ambiguities.*

(a) *Meaning one:* He waited by the financial building.
Meaning two: He waited by the shore.

(b) *Meaning one:* Is he really that type?
Meaning two: Is he really that compassionate?

(c) *Meaning one:* The proprietor of the fish store owned the sole.
Meaning two: The proprietor of the fish store was the only owner.

(d) *Meaning one:* The tool was boring a hole.
Meaning two: The long exercise was dull.

(e) *Meaning one:* It was good of him to get the title to the land.

Meaning two: The clear title to the land was valid.

(f) *Meaning one:* It takes a good straightedge to make a straight line.

Meaning two: It takes a good monarch to make a straight line.

(g) *Meaning one:* He saw that can of gasoline explode.

Meaning two: He saw that it's possible for gasoline to explode.

3. *Intonational disambiguation.* The sentences that can be disambiguated using intonation are (b), (c), (d), and (e).

4. *Complementary, gradable, and relational opposites.*

A	B	C
good	bad	g
expensive	cheap	g
parent	offspring	r
beautiful	ugly	g
false	true	c
lessor	lessee	r
pass	fail	c
hot	cold	g
legal	illegal	c
larger	smaller	r
poor	rich	g
fast	slow	g
asleep	awake	c
husband	wife	r
rude	polite	g

5. *Thematic relations.*

(a)
     a   t   l
Mary found a ball in the house.

(b)
        a   s
The children ran from the playground

        g
to the wading pool.

(c)
        a   t
One of the men unlocked all the doors

        i
with a paperclip.

(d)
    a   t   i
John   melted the   ice   with a   blowtorch.

(e)
       i   t
The   sun   melted the   ice.

(f)
      t
The   ice   melted.

(g)
        t   i
Broken   ice   still melts in the   sun.

(h)
              a   t   g
The farmer's   daughter   loaded   hay   onto the   truck.

(i)
              a   t
The farmer's   daughter   loaded the   hay
               i
with a   pitchfork.

(j)
      t   g   a
The   hay   was loaded onto the   truck   by the   farmer.

6. *Non-agentive subjects.* Here are sample answers:

fall: (The rock fell.) — theme

give: (She gave me a quarter.) — source

break: (The rock broke the glass.) — instrument

attract: (The noise attracted a crowd.) — goal

interest: (This project interests me.) — theme

7. *Analytic vs. circumstantial truth.*

(a) Queens are monarchs.	A
(b) Queens are female.	A
(c) Queens are mothers.	T
(d) Dogs are four-legged.	T
(e) Dogs are animals.	A
(f) Cats are felines.	A
(g) Cats are stupid.	T
(h) George Washington is George Washington.	A
(i) George Washington was the first president.	T
(j) Uncles are male.	A

8. *Contradiction vs. circumstantial falsehood.*

    (a) My aunt is a man.   C

    (b) Witches are wicked.   F

    (c) My brother is an only child.   C

    (d) The evening star isn't the morning star.   F

    (e) The evening star isn't the evening star.   C

    (f) Babies are adults.   C

    (g) Babies can lift one ton.   F

    (h) Puppies are human.   C

    (i) My bachelor friends are all married.   C

    (j) My bachelor friends are all lonely.   F

9. *Performatives.*

    (a) In a game of tag, someone becomes "it" when the person who is currently "it" touches him/her and shouts "you're it!"

    (b) A person becomes a knight when the Queen says "I dub thee Sir Rodney."

    (c) In Scrabble, you can challenge the validity of a word by saying "I challenge."

    (d) Two people are married when the preacher says "I hereby pronounce you husband and wife."

    (e) In card games like pinochle, the bidding is opened when the dealer says "The bid is open."

10. *Performance sentences.* The performance sentences are (c), (g), (i), (k), (m).

11. *Presuppositions.*

    (a) Presupposition: The minors were drinking.

    (b) Presupposition: You have taken me out to the ball game before.

    (c) Presupposition: Valerie did not receive a new T-bird for Labor Day.

    (d) Presupposition: Emily's pet turtle ran away.

    (e) Presupposition: The professors support the students.

    (f) Presupposition: The U.S. invaded Cambodia in 1970.

    (g) Presupposition: The U.S. invaded Cambodia in 1970.

(h) Presupposition: Disa has had some popcorn already.

(i) Presupposition: Pigs don't have wings.

(j) Presupposition: Somebody discovered America in 1492.

12. *Sentence interpretation; presupposition.*

    A. (1) red
       (2) Czolgosz shot McKinley.
       (3) Cinna stabbed Caesar.
       (4) Sam was exhausted.

    B. (5) T
       (6) F
       (7) T
       (8) F
       (9) T

13. *Deictic expressions.* Expressions to be circled in the exercise are italicized below.

(a) *I* saw *her* standing *there.*

(b) Dogs are animals.

(c) *Yesterday,* all *my* troubles seemed so *far away.*

(d) The name of *this* rock band is "The Beatles."

(e) The Declaration of Independence was signed in 1776.

(f) The Declaration of Independence was signed *last* year.

(g) Copper conducts electricity.

(h) The treasure chest is on the *right.*

(i) *These* are the times that try men's souls.

(j) There is a tide in the affairs of men which taken at the flood leads on to fortune.

14. *Pronouns.* The following judgments are based on the assumptions that *John* refers to a male, and *Maria* to a female.

(a) herself – bound; I – free

(b) he – free; her – bound or free

(c) I – free; you – free; her – free

(d) himself – bound; him – bound or free; her – free

(e) it – expletive (bound); she – free; he – free; them – free

(f) their own – bound

15. *Homonymy and polysemy.* Here are sample answers, five sets each of homonymous and polysemous words. Only the first three or four words or meanings in each set are listed, and the definitions given in the dictionary are abbreviated.

Homonyms.

(a) **fit**[1]: adapted or suited, appropriate.

fit[2]: a sudden, acute attack or manifestation of a disease, esp. one marked by convulsions or unconsciousness.

fit[3]: *Archaic.* a song, ballad, or story.

fit[4]: *Nonstandard.* pt. of **fight**.

(b) **lay**[1]: to put or place in a horizontal position or position of rest.

lay[2]: pt. of **lie**.

lay[3]: belonging to, pertaining to, or performed by the people or laity, as distinguished from the clergy.

lay[4]: a short narrative or other poem, esp. one to be sung.

(c) **low**[1]: situated, placed, or occurring not far above the ground, floor, or base.

low[2]: to utter the deep, low sound characteristic of cattle, moo.

low[3]: *Brit. Dial.* to burn, blaze.

(d) **mat**[1]: a piece of fabric made of plaited or woven rushes, straw, hemp, or similar fiber ... used as a protective covering ... to wipe the shoes on, etc.

mat[2]: a piece of cardboard or other material placed over or under a drawing, painting, etc. to serve as a frame or border.

mat[3]: matte.

mat[4]: the intaglio, usually of papier-mâché, ... from which a stereotype plate is cast.

(e) **port**[1]: a city, town, or other place where ships load or unload.

port[2]: the left-hand side of a vessel or aircraft, facing forward.

port[3]: any of a class of very sweet wines, mostly dark red, originally from Portugal.

port[4]: an opening in the side ... of a ship for admitting air and light.

(f) **scale**[1]: *Zool.* one of the thin, flat, horny plates forming the covering of certain animals.

scale[2]: a balance ... or other devices for weighing.

scale[3]: a succession or progression of steps or degrees.

37

Polysemous Words:

(a) **bark**: 1. the abrupt, harsh, explosive cry of a dog.

2. a similar sound made by another animal, such as a fox.

3. a short, explosive sound, as of firearms.

4. a brusque order, reply, etc.

(b) **fire**: 1. a state, process, or instance of combustion.

2. a burning mass of material.

3. the destructive burning of a building, town, forest, etc.

4. heat used for cooking.

(c) **fresh**: 1. newly made or obtained.

2. recently arrived, just come.

3. new, not previously known; novel.

4. additional or further.

5. not salty, as water.

(d) **knock**: 1. to strike a sounding blow with the fist, knuckles, or anything hard, esp. on a door, window ...in seeking admittance ...or giving a signal.

2. to strike in collision, bump.

3. to make a pounding noise.

4. *Informal.* to engage in trivial or carping criticism; find fault.

(e) **relative**: 1. a person who is connected with another or others by blood or marriage.

2. something having, or standing in, some relation to something else.

3. something dependent upon external conditions for its specific nature, size, etc.

4. *Gram.* a relative pronoun, adjective, or adverb.

16. *Ambiguity; paraphrases.*

(a) *We laughed at the colorful ball.*

i. At the colorful dance, we laughed.

ii. We found the colorful dance amusing.

iii. We found the colorful toy amusing.

(b) *He was knocked over by the punch.*

i. He was intoxicated by the fruit drink.

ii. He was physically knocked over by the punch bowl.

iii. He was knocked over by a punch from someone's fist.

38

(c) *The police were urged to stop drinking by the fifth.*

    i. The police were urged to quit drinking whole fifths of liquor.

    ii. The police were urged to quit drinking alcohol by the fifth of the month.

    iii. The police were urged to stop people from drinking whole fifths of liquor.

    iv. The police were urged to stop people from drinking liquor by the fifth of the month.

(d) *I said I would file it on Thursday.*

    i. I said Thursday I would put it in the file.

    ii. I said Thursday I would file it down using a rasp.

    iii. I said that Thursday I would put it in the file.

    iv. I said that Thursday I would file it down using a rasp.

(e) *I cannot recommend visiting professors too highly.*

    i. I strongly recommend that you visit professors.

    ii. I do not recommend that you visit professors.

    iii. I strongly recommend professors who are visiting.

    iv. I do not recommend professors who are visiting.

(f) *The license fee for pets owned by senior citizens who have not been altered is $1.50.*

    i. The license fee for pets owned by unaltered senior citizens is $1.50.

    ii. The license fee for unaltered pets owned by senior citizens is $1.50.

(g) *What looks better on a handsome man than a tux? Nothing!*

    i. A handsome man looks better when he's wearing a tux than when he's wearing anything else.

    ii. A handsome man looks better when he's wearing nothing than when he's wearing a tux.

Chapter 5

Phonetics

1. *Initial sound.*

a. judge	[j]		f. thought	[θ]
b. Thomas	[tʰ]		g. contact	[kʰ]
c. though	[ð]		h. phone	[f]
d. easy	[i]		i. civic	[s]
e. pneumonia	[n]		j. usury	[j]

2. *Final sound.*

a. fleece	[s]		f. cow	[aw]
b. neigh	[e]		g. rough	[f]
c. long	[ŋ]		h. cheese	[z]
d. health	[θ]		i. bleached	[t]
e. watch	[č]		j. rags	[z]

3. *Phonetic transcription.* Note: transcriptions will vary across dialects. For example, the *marry–merry–Mary* distinction is neutralized in many dialects.

a. physics	[fɪzɪks]		f. marry	[mæri]
b. merry	[mɛri]		g. tease	[tʰiz]
c. weather	[wɛðər]		h. heath	[hiθ]
d. coat	[kʰot]		i. Mary	[mɛri]
e. yellow	[jɛlo]		j. (student's name)	[kʰɛrə̃n]

41

4. *Correcting major errors in transcription.*

a. cÃm	should be	kʰÃm
b. sed	should be	sɛd
c. tʰɔlk	should be	tʰɔk
d. ãnd	should be	ǽnd
e. wæx	should be	wæks
f. kʰæbəgəz	should be	kʰæbəǰəz
g. ɪs	should be	ɪz
h. wɛθər	should be	wɛðər

5. *Symbol for phonetic descriptions.*

    (a) [p]: *spill*

    (b) [æ]: *cat*

    (c) [l]: *like*

    (d) [ŋ]: *sing*

    (e) [ð]: *other*

    (f) [č]: *church*

    (g) [j]: *yes*

    (h) [ɛ]: *red*

    (i) [u]: *cool*

6. *Phonetic properties.*

    (a) bath–bathe: The **th** in *bath* is voiceless; the **th** in *bathe* is voiced. Both are interdental fricatives.

    (b) reduce–reduction: The **c** in *reduce* is an alveolar fricative; the **c** in *reduction* is a velar stop. Both are voiceless obstruents.

    (c) cool–cold: The **oo** in *cool* is high; the **o** in *cold* is mid. Both are tense, back, and rounded.

    (d) wife–wives: The **f** in *wife* is voiceless; the **v** in *wives* is voiced. Both are labiodental fricatives.

    (e) cats–dogs: The **s** in *cats* is voiceless; the **s** in *dogs* is voiced. Both are alveolar fricatives.

    (f) impolite–indecent: The **m** in *impolite* is bilabial; the **n** in *indecent* is alveolar. Both are nasals.

7. *Transcription.*

Word	Transcription	Alternates
know	no	
tough	tʰʌf	
bough	baw	
cough	kʰaf	kʰɔf
dough	do	
you	ju	
hiccough	hɪkəp	
thorough	θəro	θərə, θr̩o
slough	slʌf	sla, slɔ
through	θru	
heard	hərd	hr̩d
word	wərd	wr̩d
beard	bird	
bird	bərd	br̩d
dead	dɛd	
said	sɛd	
bed	bɛd	
bead	bid	
deed	did	
meat	mit	
great	gret	
threat	θrɛt	
suite	swit	
straight	stret	
debt	dɛt	
moth	maθ	mɔθ
mother	mʌðər	mʌðr̩
both	boθ	
bother	baðər	baðr̩
broth	braθ	brɔθ
brother	brʌðər	brʌðr̩

8. *Shared features.*

   (a) stop, consonant

   (b) back, round, non-low, vowel

   (c) front, vowel

   (d) voiceless, consonant

   (e) voiced, consonant

   (f) coronal, consonant

9. *Matching sounds with phonetic properties.*

[u]: 5, 8

[θ]: 3, 7

[s]: 3, 7

[b]: 4, 6, 10

[l]: 3, 9

[t]: 3, 4, 6, 7

[a]: 8

[m]: 2, 4, 6, 10

10. *Translating phonetics to spelling.*

(a) Noam Chomsky is a linguist who teaches at MIT.

(b) Phonetics is the study of speech sounds.

(c) All languages use sounds produced by the upper respiratory system.

(d) In one dialect of English *cot* the noun and *caught* the verb are pronounced the same.

(e) Some people think phonetics is very interesting.

(f) Victoria Fromkin and Robert Rodman are the authors of this textbook.

11. *Phonetic features distinguishing sets of sounds.*

(a) back

(b) voicing

(c) labial

(d) high

(e) continuant

(f) obstruent

(g) back

Chapter 6

Phonology

1. *Korean.* [r] and [l] are allophones of one phoneme. They are in complementary distribution: [r] occurs syllable-initially, and [l] occurs syllable-finally. (Alternatively, [r] occurs before vowels, and [l] occurs before consonants or the end of the word.) The rule can be written as follows:

$$/l/ \rightarrow \begin{matrix} [l] & / \underline{\hspace{1em}} \left\{ \begin{matrix} C \\ \# \end{matrix} \right\} \\ [r] & / \underline{\hspace{1em}} V \end{matrix}$$

2. *Southern Kongo.*

   (a) Distributions:

   [t]–[č]: [t] occurs before the back vowels [o, a, u]; [č] occurs before [i].

   [s]–[š]: [s] occurs before [o], [u], and [e]; [š] occurs before [i].

   [z]–[ž]: [z] occurs before [u], [e], and [w]; [ž] occurs before [i].

   (b) In each pair, the nonpalatal segment should be used as the basic phoneme (e.g., [t] and [č] derived from /t/). Non-palatal segments have a wider distribution, so the rule will be simpler with the nonpalatal segment as the "elsewhere" (default) case.

   (c)
   $$\begin{bmatrix} +\text{consonantal} \\ -\text{sonorant} \\ +\text{coronal} \\ +\text{anterior} \end{bmatrix} \rightarrow [-\text{anterior}] \Big/ \underline{\hspace{1em}} \begin{bmatrix} +\text{syllabic} \\ +\text{high} \\ -\text{back} \end{bmatrix}$$

45

3. *English [aj] — [ʌj].*

(a) The sounds that end the words in columns A and B are all consonants ([+consonantal]).

(b) The words in column C end in a vowel.

(c) Yes. The distribution of [ʌj] and [aj] is predictable: [ʌj] occurs before voiceless segments, and [aj] occurs before voiced segments or word-finally.

(d) They should be derived from /aj/. [aj] has a wider distribution. Also, it is easier to characterize the distribution of [ʌj] than the distribution of [aj], so the rule will be simpler if [aj] is the sound occurring "elsewhere".

(e) life [lʌjf]   lives [lajvz]   lie [laj]
    file [fajl]   bike [bʌjk]   lice [lʌjs]

(f) /aj/ → [ʌj]/ _____ [−voice]

4. *English palatalization.* Palatalization occurs whenever these sounds (/t/, /d/, /s/, and /z/, all alveolar obstruents) are followed by the palatal glide /j/. In feature notation:

$$
\begin{bmatrix} +\text{consonantal} \\ -\text{sonorant} \\ +\text{coronal} \\ +\text{anterior} \end{bmatrix} \rightarrow [-\text{anterior}] \Big/ \underline{\hspace{1cm}} \begin{bmatrix} -\text{consonantal} \\ -\text{syllabic} \\ +\text{coronal} \\ -\text{anterior} \end{bmatrix}
$$

5. *Minimal pairs.* Students should be warned that a word's spelling often does not reflect its pronunciation, and is irrelevant in this problem. The words below are sample answers.

		Initial	Medial	Final
a.	/k/−/g/	cold/gold	mucky/muggy	tug/tuck
b.	/m/−/n/	mice/nice	simmer/sinner	sum/sun
c.	/l/−/r/	lake/rake	cold/cord	fall/far
d.	/b/−/v/	ban/van	saber/saver	dub/dove
e.	/b/−/m/	ban/man	clabber/clamor	rub/rum
f.	/p/−/f/	pail/fail	copy/coffee	leap/leaf
g.	/s/−/š/	sell/shell	masses/mashes	lease/leash
h.	/č/−/ǰ/	chin/gin	etches/edges	rich/ridge
i.	/s/−/z/	sip/zip	fussy/fuzzy	mace/maze

46

6. *Japanese.*

   (a) Yes.

   (b) [č] occurs before [i], [ts] occurs before [u], and [t] occurs elsewhere
   (before nonhigh vowels). In features: [č] occurs before [+syllabic,
   +high, −back] segments; [ts] occurs before [+syllabic, +high, +back]
   segments; and [t] occurs before [+syllabic, −high] segments (elsewhere).

   (c) [t], [ts], and [č] are allophones of a single phoneme, which we will
   represent with /t/ since the [t] allophone has the widest distribution
   of the three. The allophones are derived according to the rule below:

$$/t/ \rightarrow \begin{array}{lll} [č] & /\underline{\quad} & [+\text{syllabic}, +\text{high}, -\text{back}] \\ [ts] & /\underline{\quad} & [+\text{syllabic}, +\text{high}, +\text{back}] \\ [t] & /\underline{\quad} & [+\text{syllabic}, -\text{high}] \end{array}$$

   (d) /tatami/   /tukue/   /tutumu/
       /tomodati/ /tetudau/   /tizu/
       /uti/   /shita/   /kata/
       /tegami/   /ato/   /koto/
       /totemo/   /matu/   /tatemono/
       /otoko/   /deguti/   /te/
       /hiti/   /natu/   /turi/

7. *English stress.*

   (a) Transcription:

A	B	C
əstanıš	kəlæps	ɛksplen
ɛksıt	ɛgzıst	ires
ımæ̆jın	tormɛnt	sərprajz
kænsəl	rivolt	kʌmbajn
ilısıt	ədapt	kərin
præktıs	ınsıst	əton
səlısıt	kʌntort	ikwet

   (b) The final syllable of the verb is stressed if it ends with a consonant
   cluster; otherwise, stress the penultimate syllable.

$$V \rightarrow [+\text{stress}] \Big/ \underline{\quad} \left\{ \begin{array}{c} CC\# \\ C_0VC\# \end{array} \right\}$$

   A vowel is stressed when (a) it precedes two consonants followed by a
   word boundary, or (b) if it precedes a syllable in which there is only

one consonant followed by a word boundary. Note that the second expansion applies only if the first one does not (they are ordered disjunctively). The rule cannot apply twice to the same word.

(c) All the final vowels in column C are tense vowels. Thus, change the rule to read: Stress the final vowel of a word if it is tense or followed by a consonant cluster; otherwise stress the penultimate vowel.

$$V \rightarrow [+\text{stress}] \bigg/ \left\{ \begin{array}{ll} \overline{} \quad [+\text{tense}] & C_0\# \\ \\ \underline{} & CC\# \\ \underline{} & C_0VC\# \end{array} \right\}$$

8. *English phonotactics (sequential constraints).*

		Word	Possible	Foreign	Reason
a.	[pʰril]		X		
b.	[skrič]	screech			
c.	[know]			X	No English word begins with a stop + nasal cluster.
d.	[may]	my			
e.	[gnostɪk]			X	Same as (c).
f.	[junəkɔrn]	unicorn			
g.	[fruit]			X	In English, a glide is always inserted between front and back high vowels.
h.	[blaft]		X		
i.	[ŋar]			X	English does not have word-initial velar nasals.
j.	[æpəpʰlɛksi]	apoplexy			

9. *Finnish.*

(1) No.

(2) Yes.

(3) The sounds in neither pair are in complementary distribution.

(4) [s] and [z] are in free variation; [d] and [t] are separate phonemes.

48

(5) [s] and [z] occur in the same words freely, as shown by the pairs [liːsa] – [liːza] 'Lisa' and [kuːzi] – [kuːsi] 'six'. [d] and [t] are separate phonemes, occurring in the same environments in different words, as shown by the minimal pairs [madon] 'of a worm' – [maton] 'of a rug' and [kate] 'cover' – [kade] 'envious'.

10. *Greek.* [k] and [x] contrast, as shown by minimal pairs like [kano] – [xano]. [c] and [ç] contrast, as shown by minimal pairs like [cino] – [çino].

The velar sounds are in complementary distribution with the palatal ones. The velars [x] and [k] occur before back vowels, and the palatals [c] and [ç] occur before front vowels.

11. *Paku.*

   (1) Yes. Stress falls on the penultimate (next to last) syllable.

   (2) Nasalization is not a distinctive feature for vowels. It is predictable. A vowel is nasalized if it precedes a nasal consonant.

12. *Hebrew.*

   (a) Yes, they are in complementary distribution: [v] occurs only after vowels, [b] occurs word-initially and after consonants.

   (b) Yes; [f] occurs only after vowels, [p] occurs word-initially and after consonants.

   (c) The correct statement is (1): [b] but not [v] could occur in the empty slot.

   (d) The correct statement is (2): [p] but not [f] could occur in the empty slot.

   (e) The correct statement is (1). These words would force you to revise conclusions reached on the basis of the first group of words, since they show [b] occurring after a vowel, [v] occurring after a consonant, and [f] occurring word-initially. If the statements in (b) were correct, these words would be impossible.

13. *Maninka.*

   (a) (1) li   (2) ni

   (b) Yes. The form is *ni* if the last consonant of the stem is a nasal and *li* otherwise. Notice that the last consonant of the stem is not always the last segment of the stem.

dali	'lying down'
menni	'hearing'
famuni	'understanding'
sunogoli	'sleeping'

14. *Luganda.*

    (a) *Are nasal vowels in Luganda phonemic?* No.

        Are they predictable? Yes. Vowels are nasalized before nasal consonants.

    (b) Yes.

    (c) /ato/

    (d) No. They represent separate phonemes. While there are no minimal pairs, both [p] and [b] occur before [i] and after [a]; their distribution is not predictable.

    (e) No, because a voiced stop assimilates in nasality to a preceding nasal. Sequences of nasal consonant followed by voiced oral consonants do not occur.

    (f) Yes.

    (g) Phonemic: /enpoobe/   Phonetic: [ẽmpoobe]

    (h) The answer is (1) /en/.

    (i) [ẽntabi]

    (j) /akaugeni/

    (k) i. Vowel Nasalization: a vowel is nasalized when it precedes a nasal consonant.

        ii. Homorganic Nasal Rule: /n/ assimilates to the place of articulation of a following consonant.

       iii. Voiced Stop Assimilation: A voiced stop becomes a nasal if preceded by a nasal consonant.

Chapter 7

Language in Society

1. *Variation in English.* The nature of this problem is such that answers will vary considerably. The rightmost transcriptions are from one dialect of American English.

	Word	Transcriptions		Word	Transcriptions	
a.	horse	[hɔrs]	[hors]	hoarse	[hors]	(same)
b.	morning	[mɔrnĩŋ]	[mornĩŋ]	mourning	[mornĩŋ]	(same)
c.	for	[fɔr]	[for]	four	[for]	(same)
d.	ice	[ʌjs]	[ajs]	eyes	[ajz]	(same)
e.	knife	[nʌjf]	[nayf]	knives	[nayvz]	(same)
f.	mute	[mjut]	(same)	nude	[njud]	[nud]
g.	din	[dɪn]	(same)	den	[dɛ̃n]	(same)
h.	hog	[hɔg]	[hag]	hot	[hat]	(same)
i.	marry	[mæri]	[mɛri]	Mary	[meri]	[mɛri]
j.	merry	[mɛri]	(same)	marry	[mæri]	[mɛri]
k.	rot	[rat]	(same)	wrought	[rɔt]	(same)
l.	lease	[lis]	(same)	grease (v.)	[griz]	[gris]
m.	what	[ʌat]	[wət]	watt	[wat]	(same)
n.	ant	[æ̃nt]	(same)	aunt	[ãnt]	[æ̃nt]
o.	creek	[kʰrɪk]	[kʰrik]	creak	[kʰrik]	(same)

2. *Cameroon English Pidgin and Standard American English.*

Some Similarities: Many of the words in the CEP passage are derived from English words, such as *tok* 'talk', *gud* 'good', *nuus* 'news'. The word order seems to be SVO, as in English: *mek yi rud tret* 'make his road straight'. CEP has prepositional phrases, as English does: *bifo yoa fes* 'before your face'.

Some Differences: Some of the words in CEP are taken from the language of Cameroon rather than English; for example, *nchinda* 'prophet'. In CEP, the word *yi* indicates possession (*God yi nchinda* 'God's prophet'), while in SAE either *'s* or a PP with *of* is used. Many sounds of SAE do not exist in CEP; for example, SAE *th* ([ð]) is *d* in CEP (*di – the*), and the word-final *r* of SAE is deleted in CEP (*weh* 'where'). Also, the cluster *str* is simplified in CEP to *tr* in the word *tret* 'straight'. The SAE indefinite article *a* is replaced by *som* in CEP.

3. *American slang.* Answers will vary quite a lot depending on dialect and age. Note that in the answers given below, part (1) answers whether or not the word or phrase still exists *with its idiomatic meaning.* For example, *pipe layer* no longer has an idiomatic meaning, so the answer to part (1) for that item is 'no', even though the word still has its literal sense.

- *all out* (completely): (1) Yes; (3) *All out* still means 'completely', but is more restricted in use; the phrase *all out the best* does not occur in modern speech. Phrases like *go all out* are common, but *all out* occurs only with a small set of verbs (*go, play, run*).
- *to have apartments to let* (be an idiot): (1) No; (2) *the lights are on but nobody's home; there's nothing upstairs; not playing with a full deck*
- *been there* (experienced): (1) Yes.
- *belly-button* (navel): (1) Yes.
- *berkeleys* (a woman's breasts): (1) No; (2) *knockers, tits, boobs.*
- *bitch* (offensive name for a woman): (1) Yes.
- *once in a blue moon* (extremely seldom): (1) Yes.
- *boss* (master): (1) Yes.
- *bread* (employment): (1) Yes; (3) *Bread* as a slang term now refers to money rather than employment.
- *claim* (steal): (1) No; (2) *rip off, cop, lift.*
- *cut dirt* (escape): (1) No; (2) *take a powder* (becoming archaic), *skip out, fly the coop, make a break for it.*

- *dog cheap* (of little worth): (1) No; (2) *peanuts, dirt, diddly.*

- *funeral* (business): (1) Yes; (3) *funeral* still has an idiomatic sense in phrases like *It's your funeral,* but instead of just meaning 'it's your business', it means something like 'it's your business, but you're making a mistake.'

- *to get over* (seduce, fascinate): (1) Yes; (3) This now means 'recover', as in *I'll get over it.*

- *groovy* (settled, limited): (1) Yes; (3) 'really good, great'; in modern slang usage it is sometimes used jokingly and regarded as archaic (old slang).

- *grub* (food): (1) Yes, by some speakers; (2) *chow, munchies.*

- *head* (toilet, nautical): (1) Yes; (3) No longer restricted to nautical use.

- *hook* (marry): (1) Yes; (2) also *tie the knot, get hitched.*

- *hump* (spoil): (1) Yes; (3) have sexual intercourse.

- *hush money* (blackmail): (1) Yes.

- *itch* (be sexually excited): (1) Yes.

- *jam* (sweetheart): (1) No; (2) *baby, squeeze (old slang)*; (3) *jam* is now also a verb meaning *go, leave, split.*

- *leg bags* (stockings): (1) No; (2) *nylons.*

- *to lie low* (bide time): (1) Yes.

- *to lift a leg on* (have sexual intercourse): (1) No; (2) *get laid, get it on, do it, make it (and a zillion others).*

- *looby* (a fool): (1) No; (2) *dork, geek, nerd.*

- *malady of France* (syphilis): (1) No; (2) *clap, VD.*

- *nix* (nothing): (1) Yes; (3) This can mean 'nothing' or just 'no' (a negative command or answer).

- *noddle* (the head): (1) No; (2) *noodle, noggin, bean.*

- *old* (money): (1) No; (2) *bread, dough, bucks, moolah,* or just *cash.*

- *to pill* (talk platitudes): (1) Yes; (3) There is no slang expression that we know of that even comes close to the interpretation given. However, there is an (old) slang noun *pill* 'someone who is hard to get along with, a bother'. The noun phrase *the pill* can refers to birth control pills.

- *pipe layer* (political intriguer, schemer): (1) No; (2) There's no current equivalent that we know of, although one might suggest the noun *politicker*, or the verb phrase *play politics.*

- *poky* (cramped, stuffy, stupid): (1) Yes; (3) *pokey* can also mean jail.
- *pot* (quart, large sum, prize, urinal, excel): (1) Yes; (3) *pot* can still mean 'large sum' or 'communal money', 'prize', or 'urinal', but not 'quart' or 'excel'; it can also mean 'marijuana'.
- *puny* (freshman): (1) Yes; (3) pejorative term meaning 'small'.
- *puss-gentleman* (effeminate): (1) No; (2) *nelly, queen.*

4. Sample answers:

   (a) *jam*: go, split, leave in a hurry.

   (b) *chill*: cool down, stop acting excited.

   (c) *gnarly*: big, difficult, or great.

   (d) *pull an all-nighter*: stay up all night (studying).

   (e) *catch some Z's*: get some sleep.

   (f) *hit the books*: study.

   (g) *jazzed, stoked*: excited, elated.

   (h) *(total) bummer*: bad news, unfortunate event.

   (i) *bummed (out)*: unhappy, depressed.

   (j) *hang a louie*: make a left turn.

5. British — American equivalents.

	British		**American**
a.	clothes peg	S.	clothes pin
b.	braces	F.	suspenders
c.	lift	L.	elevator
d.	pram	K.	baby buggy
e.	waistcoat	Q.	vest
f.	shop assistant	T.	clerk
g.	sweets	A.	candy
h.	boot (of car)	P.	trunk
i.	bobby	N.	cop
j.	spanner	G.	wrench
k.	biscuits	E.	crackers
l.	queue	C.	line
m.	torch	H.	flashlight
n.	underground	R.	subway
o.	high street	D.	main street
p.	crisps	I.	potato chips

q.	lorry	B.	truck
r.	holiday	J.	vacation
s.	tin	M.	can
t.	knock up	O.	wake up

6. *Pig Latin.*

A. (1) Dialect 1: Suffix [me] to any vowel-initial word.
   Dialect 2: Suffix [he] to any vowel-initial word.
   Dialect 3: Suffix [e] to any vowel-initial word.

    (2) Phonetic transcriptions:

honest	1. [anəstme]	2. [anəsthe]	3. [anəste]
admire	1. [ædmajrme]	2. [ædmajrhe]	3. [ædmajre]
illegal	1. [ɪligəlme]	2. [ɪligəlhe]	3. [ɪligəle]

B. (1) Dialect 1: Take all the initial consonants from the first syllable of the word, add [e], and suffix the resulting syllable to the end of the word.
   Dialect 2: Take only the first consonant from the first syllable of the word add [e], and suffix the resulting syllable to the end of the word.

    (2) Phonetic transcriptions for two dialects:

	1	2
spot	[atspe]	[patse]
crisis	[ajsəskre]	[rajsəske]
scratch	[æčskre]	[kræčse]

7. *Other English language games.*

(a) /aj tʊk maj dɔg awtsajd/ (I took my dog outside).
   The rule is to suffix [o] to each syllable.

(b) /hir ɪz ə mɔr kamplɪketəd gem/ (here is a more complicated game).
   The rule is to suffix [li] after each syllable.

(c) Mary can talk in rhyme.
   The rule is to replace the initial consonants (if any) of each word with [shm] and suffix the result to the original.

(d) Better late than never.
   The rule is to replace the initial consonants (if any) of each syllable with [p] and suffix the result to the original.

(e) /ðə futbal stediəm blu dawn/ (the football stadium blew down).
The rule is to insert [ap] (*op*) after the initial consonant (cluster) of each syllable.

(f) /kən ju spik ðɪs kajnd ʌv ɪŋglɪš/ (can you speak this kind of English).
The rule is to insert the stressed syllable [*áb*] after the initial consonant (cluster) of each syllable.

8. *Jargon.* Answers to this exercise will naturally vary according to the profession or trade the student chooses to represent. The jargon listed here for a sample answer is taken from the field of academic professors at the University of California.

(a) chair (or chairman or chairwoman) – the head of a department

(b) CV – Curriculum Vitae, the academic résumé

(c) the Senate – Academic Senate, a body of University faculty which makes policy decisions for the University.

(d) ladder – in a position to advance within the University hierarchy of professorship.

(e) AA – Administrative Assistant

(f) RA – Research Assistant

(g) TA – Teaching Assistant

(h) post-doc (post-doctoral) – a temporary job (usually one year) in research or teaching for someone who has just completed a doctorate.

(i) ABD – All-But-Dissertation: adjective describing a student who has finished everything for a Ph.D. except a dissertation.

(j) sabbatical – paid leave of absence, usually one year long, after six years of teaching.

(k) FTE – Full Time Equivalency: a full time academic position within a department of the University.

9. *Formal — colloquial translation.* Here is a sample "translation" of the first paragraph of the Declaration of Independence. There are varying degrees of informality in style that could be used in doing this exercise.

> When a group of people wants to break away from another group and form their own country (which they should be entitled to do), they ought to say clearly what motivated the separation if they have any respect for the opinion of the rest of the world.

Chapter 8

Language Change

1. *Old English: sound changes.*

   (a) *crabbe* [krabə] → *crab* [kræb]
   Changes: (1) The vowel [a] became [æ]. (2) The word-final [ə] was lost.

   (b) *fisc* [fɪsk] → *fish* [fɪš]
   Changes: (1) The final [k] was lost. (2) [s] became [š].

   (c) *fūl* [fu:l] → *foul* [fawl]
   Changes: (1) The long vowel [u:] became [aw].

   (d) *gāt* [ga:t] → *goat* [got]
   Changes: (1) The long vowel [a:] became [o].

   (e) *lǣfan* [læ:van] → *leave* [liv]
   Changes: (1) The [an] ending was lost. (2) The long vowel [æ:] became [i].

   (f) *tēþ* [te:θ] → *teeth* [tiθ]
   Changes: (1) The long vowel [e:] became [i].

2. *Great Vowel Shift.* Here is a set of possible answers.

	[i]/[ɛ]	[aj]/[ɪ]	[e]/[æ]
i.	clean/cleanse	deride/derision	vain/vanity
ii.	thief/theft	rhyme/rhythm	sate/satisfy
iii.	feel/felt	crime/criminal	flame/flammable
iv.	reveal/revelation	precise/precision	nation/national
v.	please/pleasure	line/linear	page/paginate

3. *Changes in English.* In the answers given below, only syntactic changes are discussed. Lexical changes (e.g., *hath* to *has*) are ignored.

(a) *It nothing* pleased his master.

Mod. Eng.: Nothing pleased his master.

Change: In Old English the expletive subject *it* co-occurred with the logical subject (in this case, *nothing*). In Modern English this is not possible: *it* appears only when there is no other subject available.

(b) He hath said that we would lift *them whom that him please.*

Mod. Eng.: He has said that we would lift those who please him.

Changes: (1) In OE pronouns like *them* can take a relative clause, while In ModE they generally cannot—they are replaced in ModE by demonstratives like *those*. (2) In OE the WH-phrase *whom* and the complementizer *that* both occurred in the complementizer position, while in ModE only one of them may occur there. (3) In OE the object *him* can go before the verb *please*, while in ModE the verb must precede the object.

(c) I have a brother *is* condemned to die.

Mod. Eng.: I have a brother who is condemned to die.

Change: It appears that in OE a relative pronoun (the pronoun occurring in the complementizer of a relative clause) corresponding to the subject of the relative clause may be null. In ModE a subject relative pronoun cannot be null.

(d) I bade them *take away you.*

Mod. Eng.: I asked them to take you away.

Change: In OE a verb-particle pair could be followed by a pronoun. In ModE if the verb and the particle are separable, the particle must follow the object if the object is a pronoun.

(e) I wish you *was still more a Tartar.*

Mod. Eng.: I wish you were still more of a Tartar; or I wish even more that you were a Tartar.

Change: (1) The verb *be* must agree in ModE with the subject. (2) Depending on what the meaning is interpreted to be, either (a) *of* must be inserted into the phrase *more a Tartar* because *more* cannot modify a predicate nominal in ModE; or (b) the phrase "still more", modifying "wish", must precede the embedded sentence.

(f) Christ slept *and his apostles.*

Mod. Eng.: Christ slept and his apostles did too.

Change: In OE a verb phrase could be entirely missing if identical to the preceding verb phrase. In ModE an auxiliary verb (*did* in this case) must remain.

(g) *Me* was told.

Mod. Eng.: I was told.

Change: In OE the subject of a passive clause appeared with accusative case, while in ModE it must have nominative case.

4. *New and old words in English.* Here are sample answers:

(a) • *power lunch*: a business lunch in which agreements and transactions are made.

• *Reaganomics*: the style of economics practiced by the Reagan administration.

• *CD*: short for *compact disc*, a miniature analog of the hard computer disc, now used to record music. CDs are played on CD players.

• *floppy*: a small, soft diskette used to store computer documents which can be read by a computer having a floppy drive (mechanism to read the diskette). Source: from the adjective *floppy* 'soft, bendable' in the phrase *floppy disk*, now shortened to *floppy*.

• *clone*: exact duplicate of anything. Source: biological gene research.

(b) • *flapper*: 1920s term for a young woman who is bold and unconventional in her style of dress.

• *slide rule*: a handheld instrument the size of a foot-long ruler used to calculate square roots and other mathematical relations; becoming obsolete with the advances of computer technology.

• *phonograph*: record player, turntable, stereo.

5. *Latin — French correspondences.*

(a) False.

(b) True.

(c) False.

(d) True.

6. *Indo-European.* The Indo-European languages are 1, 2, 4, 8, 10, and 11.

7. *The world's languages.* The number of languages spoken in the world might grow larger as groups of people (like amoeba) split off from each other and are separated by belief, culture, or geographical boundaries. The language spoken by each group would develop independently until they are mutually incomprehensible.

The number of languages spoken in the world might grow smaller as groups of people are conquered by or merge with a more dominant or populous group. Many of the indigenous languages of the Americas have died out in this way.

The student can argue either way in answering the third part of this question, as an exercise in reasoning and writing.

8. *Etymology.* We used the Random House Dictionary of the English Language, 2nd edition (unabridged). Only the etymological information associated with each word is given below; the student may speculate freely on how each word was borrowed.

   (a) *size*: From Old French *assiser* 'assize', which has as one of its meanings 'a statute for regulating weights and measures'.

   (b) *royal*: From Middle French from Latin *regalis* 'kingly'.

   (c) *aquatic* : From Middle French from Latin *aqua* 'water' + -*āticus*.

   (d) *heavenly*: From Old English *heofenlīc*, akin to Old Norse *himinn*, Goth *himins*, Ger *Himmel*.

   (e) *skill*: From Old Norse *skil* 'distinction, difference'.

   (f) *ranch*: From Spanish *rancho* 'camp'.

   (g) *blouse*: From French *vêtement de laine blouse* 'garment of short (uncarded) wool'.

   (h) *robot*: From Czech, coined by Karel Čapek in the play R.U.R. (1920) from the base *robot-*, as in *robota* 'compulsory labor', *robotnik* 'peasant owing such labor'.

   (i) *check*: From Old French *eschec*, var. of *eschac* from Arabic *shāh* 'check' (at chess), from Persian: lit., king (an exclamation: i.e., 'look out, your king is threatened').

   (j) *banana* : From Portuguese (perhaps via Spanish); akin to various words for banana or plantain in West African languages (e.g., Wolof,

Malinke *banana* Vai *bana*, but ultimate source and direction of borrowing uncertain).

(k) *keel*: From Old English *cēol*, from Gothic *kiel* 'ship'.

(l) *fact*: From Latin *factum* 'something done, deed'.

(m) *potato*: From Spanish *patata* 'white potato', var. of *batata* 'sweet potato', from Taino.

(n) *muskrat*: Alteration by folk etymology of *musquash*, Massachusett cognate of Western Abenaki *mòskwas*.

(o) *skunk*: From the Massachusett reflex of Proto-Algonquian **šeka·kwa*, deriv. of **šek-* 'urinate' + *-a·kw* 'fox'.

(p) *catfish*: From *cat* 'cat' + *fish* 'fish' (fish resembling a cat).

(q) *hoodlum*: American, probably from dialectal German; cf. Swabian derivatives of *Hudel* 'rag', e.g., *hudelum* 'disorderly', *hudellam* 'weak, slack', etc.

(r) *filibuster*: From Spanish *filibustero* from Middle French *flibustier*, var. of *fribustier*; see FREEBOOTER.

(s) *astronaut*: From French *astronautique* ASTRO + *-naute* from Greek *naútēs* 'sailor', on the model of *aéronaute* 'aeronaut'.

(t) *emerald*: From Old French *esmeraude, esmeralde, esmeragde* from Latin *smaragdus* from Greek *smáragdos*; probably ultimately from Semitic *b–r–q* 'shine' (Sanskrit *marāk(a)la* 'emerald').

(u) *sugar*: From Middle English and Middle French *sucre*, from Middle Latin *succārum*, Italian *zucchero*, Arabic *sukkar*; obscurely akin to Persian *shakar*, Greek *sákcharon*.

(v) *pagoda*: From Portuguese *pagode* 'temple', from Persian *butkada* (*but* 'idol' + *kada* 'temple, dwelling').

(w) *khaki*: From Urdu, from Persian *khākī* 'dusty', equivalent to *khāk* 'dust' + *ī* 'suffix of appurtenance'.

(x) *shampoo*: Earlier *champo* 'to massage', from an inflected form of Hindi *cāmpnā*, lit., 'to press'.

(y) *kangaroo*: From Guugu Yimidhirr (Australian Aboriginal language spoken around Cookstown, N. Queensland) *gaŋ-urru*, large black or gray species of kangaroo.

(z) *bulldoze*: American, origin uncertain; the notion that it represents a verbal use of *bull dose*, i.e., a dose fit for a bull, is probably specious.

9. *Phobias.*

(a) *Arachibutyrophobia* 'fear of peanut butter sticking to the roof of your mouth' could be derived from a combination of *arachis oil* 'peanut oil' plus *butyraceous* 'of or resembling butter' plus *phobia* 'fear.'

(b) Examples of 'phobia' words that one might make up:
ovumtortolaphobia 'fear of turtle eggs'
facetiaphobia 'fear of jokes'
amylcollarephobia 'fear of starched collars'

10. *Analogic change.* Below is one example:

In common usage it is considered nonstandard to say *it's me, I'm her,* etc. as opposed to *it is I* or *I am she*. In standard English, pronouns in the accusative case form are typically in a noninitial position in a sentence, while subject pronouns (which are in the nominative case form) are usually initial. Speakers for whom *it's me* is well-formed have generalized (or reinterpreted) the distinction of *subject* vs. *object* to one of *initial* vs. *noninitial*.

Interestingly, after years of being told by well-meaning schoolteachers that it is incorrect to say *Susie and me* in sentences like *Susie and me are going,* many speakers would now say *Susie and I,* whether the coordinate NP is a subject or not. Such speakers might produce sentences like *he was talking to Susie and I.* Because of this, some speakers who have the initial—noninitial distinction for pronouns have a different rule for pronouns which are noninitial in a coordinate NP: they always receive nominative case.

11. *Differences from the English of* <u>Hamlet</u>.

Line 1: *hath eat of a King* is now *has eaten a King* or *has eaten King*.

Line 2: *hath fed of that worm* is now *has fed on that worm*.

Line 3: *dost thou* is now *do you*.

Line 4: *go a progress* is now *progress*.

Line 7: *thither* is now *there*.

Line 7: *find him not* is now *does not find him*.

Line 8: *i'* is no longer contractable and would be *in*.

Line 8: *find him not*: see line 7.

Line 9: *you shall* is now *you will*.

Line 9: *nose* no longer exists and would be replaced by *smell*.

12. *Historical Reconstruction.*

A.
m–m	p–p	t–t	m–w
w–w	s–s	ʔ–ʔ	n–n
h–h	k–k	u–u	i–i
a–a	ɨ–ɨ	o–o	a–e

B. i. Proto-sounds:

p–p:	*p	t–t:	*t
s–s:	*s	ʔ–ʔ:	*ʔ
n–n:	*n	h–h:	*h
k–k:	*k	u–u:	*u
i–i:	*i	a–a:	*a
ɨ–ɨ:	*ɨ	o–o:	*o
a–e:	*e		

   ii. The last item above shows a change: proto *e* became *a* in YP.

C. i. w

   ii. m, w

   iii. Yes. A YP *m* corresponds to a NM *m* word-initially and a NM *w* between vowels.

D. i. Two.

   ii. If you chose three, they would have to be *m, *w and an abstract sound representing both of them, perhaps *b. Then *m corresponds to *m* in both languages, *w corresponds to *w* in both languages, and *b corresponds to *m* word initially and *w* between vowels in NM. But this solution is unmotivated; the simpler solution below is better.

   iii. The proto-sounds are *m and *w. Proto *m becomes *m* in YP. In NM, proto *m becomes *m* word-initially and *w* between vowels. Proto *w becomes *w* in both YP and NM.

E. The proto forms are as in YP except for the words with a proto *e* sound:

*mupi	*tama	*piwɨ
*sawaʔpono	*nɨmɨ	*tamano
*pahwa	*kuma	*wowaʔa
*mɨhɨ	*noto	*tape
*ʔatapɨ	*papiʔi	*petɨ
*nana	*ʔetɨ	

63

Chapter 9

Writing

1. *Pictograms.* The following are sample answers.

   (a) *eye*:

   (b) *a boy*:

   (c) *two boys*:

   (d) *library*:

   (e) *tree*:

(f) *forest*:

(g) *war*:

(h) *honesty*:

(i) *ugly*:

(j) *run*:

(k) *Scotch tape*:

(l) *smoke*:

B. The most difficult words are abstract and subjective words like *honesty* and *ugly*, because they are hard to represent with pictures whose meanings are transparent. Also, it is difficult to represent the difference between an explicit number of things (like *two boys*) and a large group of things (like *forest* or *library*).

C. Abstract concepts such as *internalized* and *unconscious* would be difficult to portray. This is also true of relations such as *of* and *represents*.

2. *Rebuses.* Sample answers are given below.

A.

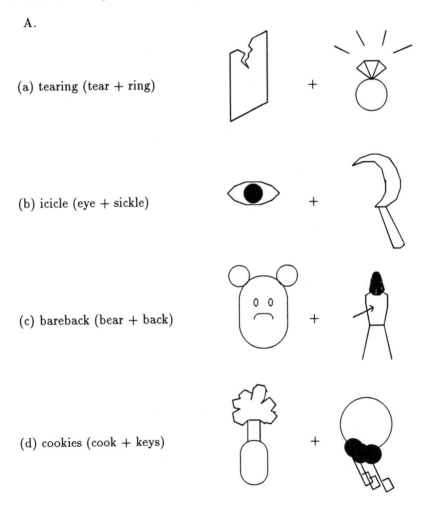

(a) tearing (tear + ring)

(b) icicle (eye + sickle)

(c) bareback (bear + back)

(d) cookies (cook + keys)

B. There would be problems with ambiguous pictures (pictures of objects with several different names, such as *chair* and *seat*). Also, it would be difficult or impossible to maintain consistency so that the same set of pictures always gives the same message. In addition, variation in pronunciation could have a disastrous effect in an attempt to understand something.

3. *Non-Roman alphabetic letters.*

A. To show how this is done, the sample answer below contains Greek letters for these sounds rather than made-up alphabetic characters. However, students should construct their own alphabetic characters.

t:	τ	r:	ρ
s:	σ	k:	κ
w:	ʋ	č:	χ
i:	ι	æ:	α
f:	φ	n:	ν

B. We have used regular alphabetic spelling (not phonetic spelling) for sounds not specified in the new orthography.

(a) *character* : καρακτερ

(b) *guest* : gueστ

(c) *cough* : κουφ

(d) *photo* : φοτο

(e) *cheat* : χιτ

(f) *rang* : ραʋg

(g) *psychotic* : σγκοτικ

(h) *tree* : τρι

4. *Syllabic systems.* Consistency is important in this exercise.

a.	childishness: ABC	g.	witness: GC
b.	childlike: AD	h.	lethal: JK
c.	Jesuit: EFG	i.	jealous: EI
d.	lifelessness: HIC	j.	witless: GI
e.	likely: DJ	k.	lesson: IL
f.	zoo: F		

Syllabary: A = child [čajld], B = ish [ɪsh], C = ness [nɛs], D = like [lajk], E = je [jɛ], F = su [zu], G = wit [wɪt], H = life [lajf], I = less or lous [lɛs], J = ly [li], K = thal [θəl], L = son [sən].

5. *Pronounced the same, spelled differently.* The key to this exercise is to think of cognates in which the letters are pronounced differently.

	A	B	Reason
a.	I am	iamb	The *b* is pronounced in words like *iambic*.
b.	goose	produce	The *c* is pronounced [k] in *production*.
c.	fashion	complication	The *t* is pronounced [t] in *complicate*.
d.	Newton	organ	The *a* is pronounced [æ] in *organic*; the *o* is pronounced [o] in *Newtonian*.
e.	no	know	The *k* is pronounced in words like *acknowledge*.
f.	hymn	him	The *n* is pronounced in *hymnal*.

6. *Spelled the same, pronounced differently.*

	A	B	Reason
a.	mingle	long	The *g* is pronounced in *longer*.
b.	line	children	There is a regular correspondence between [aj] in *child* and [ɪ] in *children*; compare *line* and *linear*.
c.	sonar	resound	The *s* is voiceless in *sound*.
d.	crumble	bomb	The *b* is pronounced in *bombadier*.
e.	cats	dogs	The voicing of the s depends only on the voicing of the preceding sound; the plural morpheme represents the sound in these cases.
f.	stagnant	design	The *g* is pronounced in *designate*.
g.	serene	obscenity	The [i] – [ɛ] alternation is predictable by phonological environment; compare *serenity*.

7. *Disambiguation through intonation.*

(a) *What are we having for dinner, Mother?*

If Mother is being asked a question, the intonation on *dinner* is falling and the intonation on *Mother* is rising. If the question is whether we are having Mother for dinner, there is a pause between *dinner* and *Mother*, there is falling intonation on *dinner*, and the rising intonation on *Mother* starts higher.

(b) *She's a German language teacher.*

If the statement is about a language teacher who is German, the main stress is on *language*. If the statement is about someone who is a teacher of the German language, main stress is on *teacher*.

(c) *They formed a student grievance committee.*
If it is a committee on student grievances, main stress is on *committee*; if it is a student committee on grievances, main stress is on *grievance*.

(d) *Charles kissed his wife and George kissed his wife too.*
If both Charles and George kissed the same person, stress is on *George* and/or *too*. If each man kissed his own wife, contrastive stress is necessary on the second instance of *his*.

8. *Disambiguation through writing.*

(a) *They're my brothers' keepers.* When the plural *-s* is followed by the possessive *-s*, only one of them is pronounced, so in spoken language a singular possessive noun sounds the same as a plural possessive noun. In written language, the apostrophe is written after the *-s* to indicate the plural possessive, and before the *-s* to indicate the singular possessive.

(b) *He said, "He will take the garbage out."* In spoken language, this could be either a direct quote or an indirect quote; in written language direct quotes are set off by quote marks, while indirect quotes are not.

(c) *The red book was read.* This sentence is ambiguous when spoken because the adjective *red* and the passive participle *read* are pronounced the same. They are spelled differently, though, so in written form the sentence is unambiguous.

(d) *The flower is on the table.* As with the item above, the different spellings of *flower* and *flour* make the sentence unambiguous when written.

9. *Identifying writing.*

(a) Cherokee – 7

(b) Chinese – 6

(c) German (Gothic style) – 9

(d) Greek – 2

(e) Hebrew – 4

(f) Icelandic – 8

(g) Japanese – 1

(h) Korean – 10

(i) Russian – 3

(j) Twi – 5

10. *Identifying languages.*

(a) Spanish

(b) English

(c) French

(d) German

(e) Italian

(f) Portuguese

(g) Japanese

(h) Russian

(i) Polish

(j) Serbo-Croatian

(k) Greek

(l) Turkish

(m) Arabic

Chapter 10

Language Acquisition

1. *Baby talk.*

   (1)

Animals	Events	People	Objects
horsey	bye-bye	mama	choo-choo
kitty	night-night	dada	jammies
piggy	boo-boo	nana	tummy
bunny	ow-ow		potty
doggie			

   (2) Rules:

   (a) A consonant cluster may be reduced: for example, [stʌmək] becomes [tʌmi]; final consonants may be dropped.

   (b) Stressless syllables may be dropped: for example, [pəǰæməz] becomes [ǰæmiz].

   (c) The diminuitive -*i* (spelled *y* or *ie*) is suffixed to a word, sometimes replacing existing syllables.

   (d) Reduplicated syllables may also replace existing syllables, as in *bye-bye* for *goodbye*.

2. *Acquiring negation.* In the acquisition of negative sentences, the child begins by adding a *no* or other negative at the beginning or end of a sentence. This could be an overgeneralization of the rule that allows some negative sentences in English to be formed with an initial *no*, as in the following:

   No, I don't want to do that.

   No, she isn't leaving.

   No, don't close the door.

When the child begins to put the negative element in second position, this reflects the realization that the negative element (attached to an auxiliary verb) can occur in second position. But the rule is overgeneralized: the bare negative element *no* or *not* is included as one of the second-position auxiliaries; *no* and *don't* have the same status in the child's grammar.

In acquiring questions, the child initially uses only question intonation to indicate that a question is being asked. This is overgeneralization: in adult speech not all questions have rising intonation. In the next stage the child forms questions by "tacking on" an initial *wh*–word at the beginning of the sentence. The child is overgeneralizing (and oversimplifying) by treating questions simply as statements with a *wh*– word in front.

4. *Comment on Chomsky's remark.* The answer to this question should reflect an understanding of the studies presented in the chapter which purport to show that the acquisition of language follows a pattern of development analogous to other kinds of biological development. The basis of the remark is in the fact that humans acquire language *without instruction*, while apes do not. The remark is also based on the assumption that communication between apes is not a language; by "language ability" Chomsky clearly means "human language ability." The analogy to flightless birds implies that learning to speak a language is like learning to fly — it is a property of the species. A species of birds that does not fly simply does not have the biological endowment to do so.

3. *Adam, Eve, and Sarah.*

    A. (1) Mini grammar (sample answer):

        i. S → V N

        ii. S → V it

        iii. S → Adj N

        iv. S → more N

        v. S → N V

        vi. S → bye-bye N

        vii. S → bye-bye Adj

    (2) Trees — sample answer. Students' trees should follow their own phrase structure rules from part (1).

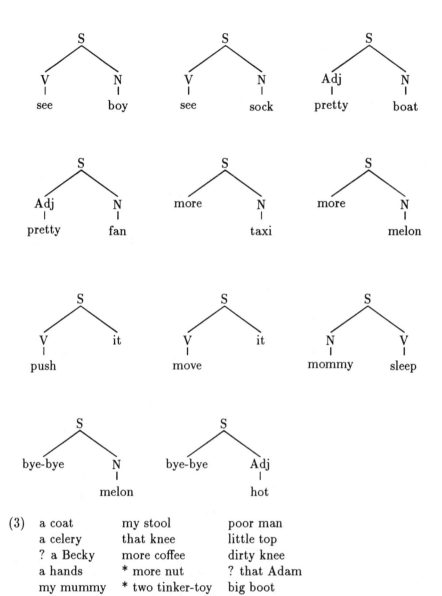

(3) a coat   my stool   poor man
     a celery   that knee   little top
     ? a Becky   more coffee   dirty knee
     a hands   * more nut   ? that Adam
     my mummy   * two tinker-toy big boot

(4) *a celery: Celery is a mass noun, and a must be followed by some-
     thing countable and singular: a piece/stalk/bite of celery.
     ?a Becky: Names, especially names of people, do not usually occur
     with determiners in English. However, note that this phrase is well-
     formed in certain contexts (e.g., My name is Becky, and I live next
     door to a Becky [someone whose name is also Becky]).
     *a hands: The article a must be followed by a singular noun.
     *more nut: More must be followed by a mass noun (coffee) or a

plural noun (*nuts*).

?that Adam: See (b), above. This phrase is also fine in certain contexts.

*two tinker-toy: Numerals greater than one must be followed by a plural (and countable) noun.

4. *Holophrastic stage phonology.*

A.

	Adult	Child	Substitution
(1)	dont	dot	final cluster [nt] reduced to single [t]
(2)	skɪp	kʰɪp	initial cluster [sk] reduced to single consonant; /k/ aspirated
(3)	šu	su	palato-alveolar fricative replaced by alveolar fricative
(4)	ðæt	dæt	interdental fricative replaced by alveolar stop
(5)	pʰle	pʰe	initial cluster [pʰl] replaced by single aspirated stop
(6)	θʌmp	dʌp	initial voiceless interdental fricative replaced by voiced alveolar stop; final [mp] cluster replaced by single [p]
(7)	bæθ	bæt	final interdental fricative replaced by voiceless alveolar stop
(8)	čap	tʰap	affricate replaced by alveolar stop
(9)	kʰɪDi	kʰɪdi	flap replaced by voiced alveolar stop
(10)	lajt	wajt	lateral liquid replaced by labiovelar glide
(11)	dali	dawi	lateral liquid replaced by labiovelar glide
(12)	gro	go	initial [gr] cluster reduced to single consonant

B. General rules for children's pronunciation (sample answer):

(a) In consonant clusters consisting of a stop and a fricative, liquid, or nasal, delete the fricative or nasal.

(b) Replace interdental fricatives with alveolar stops.

(c) Replace palato-alveolars with alveolars.

(d) Replace the lateral liquid with the labiovelar glide.

Chapter 11

Language Processing: the Human Brain and Mind

2. *How words are stored in the brain.*

A. The substituted words in group (a) are in the same syntactic category as the stimulus words and are semantically related. They are not phonologically similar. In group (b) the substituted words are for the most part derivationally related to the stimulus words, but in every case the aphasic's words are nouns, while the given word is a verb.

B. The words in these two groups show that words are organized according to semantic class and syntactic category.

3. *Aphasic language.*

(a) *There is under a horse a new sidesaddle.*
In normal language the prepositional phrase follows the noun phrase in existential sentences. Also, the preposition would be *on* in normal speech rather than *under*.

(b) *In girls we see many happy days.*
It is not clear what this sentence means. It might be a deviant form of *We girls have many happy days.*

(c) *I'll challenge a new bike.*
In nonaphasic language the verb *challenge* must take a human or abstract object (law, for example).

(d) *I surprise no new glamor.*
The verb *surprise* must also take a human object.

(e) *Is there three chairs in this room?*

In normal language, the verb of an existential sentence agrees with the displaced subject of the sentence (in this sentence, it should be *are*).

(f) *Mike and Peter is happy.*

In normal language, the verb agrees with the number of the subject NP; in the case of a coordinate NP, number is plural if the coordinator is *and*.

(g) *Bill and John likes hot dogs.*
Same as item (f).

(h) *Proliferate is a complete time about a word that is correct.*

In normal language, *proliferate* is a verb and cannot be used as the subject of a sentence. The sentence is also semantically anomalous.

(i) *Went came in better than it did before.*

In normal language, a past tense verb form such as *went* cannot be used as the subject of a sentence. The sentence is also semantically anomalous.

4. *Rules relating spelling to pronunciation.* In the patient's system of spelling-to-pronunciation, the following are true:

- Written *a* corresponds to /e/ or /æ/
- Written *e* corresponds to /ɛ/ or /i/
- Written *i* corresponds to /aj/
- Written *o* corresponds to /o/ or /ɔ/
- Written *c* corresponds to /s/
- Every letter is pronounced separately, and there is one vowel per syllable. There are no "silent" letters in this system.

In the patient's system of pronunciation-to-spelling, the same rules hold as itemized above. In addition, the sound [k] is always written K, and the plural suffix -*s*, when realized as [z], is written Z. This indicates that the patient is not doing lexical lookup or morphological analysis.

5. *Speech errors.*

(1) a. phonological consonant
    b. reversal or exchange of segments

(2) a. lexical
    b. exchange of words

(3) a. lexical
    b. exchange of words

(4) a. morphological prefix
    b. substitution of prefix with similar meaning

(5) a. phonological consonant
    b. exchange of syllable onsets (initial consonants or no consonant)

(6) a. morphological suffix
    b. substitution of suffix with similar meaning

(7) a. lexical
    b. substitution of word with similar associations (in this case, German dog → German car)

(8) a. phonological vowel
    b. exchange of segments

(9) a. phonological consonant
    b. exchange of syllable onsets

(10) a. phonological consonant
     b. replacement of initial consonant with different consonant

(11) a. phonological consonant
     b. exchange of syllable codas (syllable-final consonants)

(12) a. phonological consonant
     b. exchange of voicing properties

(13) a. phonological consonant
     b. exchange of syllable onsets; reduction of cluster following exchange derives an existing word

(14) a. morphological suffix
     b. substitution of suffix with same meaning

(15) a. inflectional morphology
     b. verb suffix attached to preposition

Chapter 12

Language Processing: Human and Machine

1. *Voiceprints.*

   - Differences in pitch: some voices are high and others are low, even within the same sex.

   - Differences in nasality: some voices seem to be more nasal than others, even in nonnasal environments.

   - Differences in timbre or quality: some voices are described as having a clear or bell-like quality, while others have a distinctly rasping quality.

   Some of these differences are due to physical characteristics of the vocal tract; for example, pitch depends partly on the size of the vocal cords. But social factors are also involved; a "nasal accent" could be learned behavior common to a community of speakers.

2. *Word-for-word translation.* Sample answers are given below. The language here is German.

   (a) The children will   eat   the fish.
       Das Kinder   werden essen das Fisch.
       Die Kinder werden den Fisch essen.

   (b) Send   the professor a   letter from your new school.
       Schicken das Professor ein Brief von Ihr   neu Schule.
       Schicken Sie dem Professor einen Brief aus Ihrer neuen Schule.

(c) The fish   will   be   eaten by   the children.
Das Fisch werden sein essen von das Kinder.
Der Fisch wird von den Kindern gegessen worden.

(d) Who   is   the person   that is   hugging   that dog?
Wer   sein das Mensch das sein umarmen das Hund?
Wer ist der Mensch, der den Hund umarmt?

(e) The   spirit   is   willing but   the flesh   is   weak.
Das Geist   sein willig   aber das Fleisch sein schwach.
Der Geist ist willig, aber das Fleisch ist schwach.

A. (a) German has several different forms for the word *the*. The one you use depends on the gender, number, and case of the accompanying noun. In this exercise, you are forced to pick one at random (we used *das* throughout).

(b) In this task you are forced to use the form of the verb you find in the dictionary (the infinitive), even if you know that German has subject-verb agreement on the verb and singular and past tense forms.

(c) There are many different German words which translate to the English word *by*; there is no way to know which of them is the correct one (if any).

(d) English *is* is not found in the dictionary because it is an inflected form and the dictionary has only infinitive verb forms. To find the corresponding word, you have to know what the infinitive is (*be*), and look up the German word for that.

(e) Even if idiomatic expression such as *The spirit is willing, but the flesh is weak* could be translated into a grammatical sentence, there is no guarantee and little chance that the result will be idiomatic in the target language.

(f) German word order in subordinate clauses is verb-final; but in English, the verb always follows the subject. A translation of a sentence like (d), which has a relative clause, cannot reflect the proper word order in German unless the ordering of words is changed.

B. A word-for-word translation from German to English would encounter the same problems with word forms and word order; and even a knowledgeable translator will have the same difficulty with word senses mentioned in part A. For example, the German translation of (e) might translate back to English as "The ghost is ready but the meat is weak."

3. *Databases.* Sample answer: A computer could be used to produce a concordance of the work, which could then be matched with the concordances of the known works of Marlowe and Shakespeare in order to discover whose work has the best match.

4. *Speech synthesis.* Sample answers:

    (a) For announcing routine items on the radio (such as the weather report), thereby relieving human announcers of these tasks.

    (b) For everyday communication by people who are unable to talk normally because of injury or defect.

    (c) For programmable talking toys or games (dolls or robots, for example).

    (d) For conveying information to people who cannot read.

    (e) For teaching the correct pronunciation of words and sentences in a foreign language.

5. *Speech recognition.* Sample answers:

    (a) For processing of radio or television reports in the gathering of information by press or intelligence organizations.

    (b) For teaching purposes: a computer that "understands" speech could be used for drills or quizzes instead of pencil and paper.

    (c) For processing and then conveying information to people who cannot hear.

    (d) For automatic translation (if a high enough level of sophistication can be achieved).

    (e) For more efficient processing or transmission of information from languages with non-Roman writing systems.

6. *Understanding and resolving ambiguity.*

(a) John gave the boys five dollars. One of them was counterfeit.

Ambiguity: "One of them" could refer to the dollars or to the boys.

Likely: "One of them" refers to the dollars.

Knowledge: Only currency can be counterfeit; "dollars" are currency, while "boys" are not.

(b) The police were asked to stop drinking in public places.

Ambiguity: The unspecified subject of "drinking" could be "the police," or it could be arbitrary.

Likely: The subject of "drinking" is arbitrary.

Knowledge: Police action usually involves controlling the behavior of members of a society, including stopping actions that are against the law, which could include "drinking in public places." It is unlikely that they would be asked to monitor their own behavior.

(c) John went to the bank to get some cash.

Ambiguity: The word "bank" could refer to a financial institution or to the sides of a river.

Likely: The word "bank" refers to a financial institution.

Knowledge: Cash is usually obtained from a financial institution, not a river.

(d) He saw the Grand Canyon flying to New York.

Ambiguity: The subject of "flying to New York" could be "he" (the one who saw the Grand Canyon in the sentence) or it could be "the Grand Canyon."

Likely: The subject of "flying to New York" is "he."

Knowledge: "The Grand Canyon" usually refers to a place, and places (being stationary) rarely fly. "He" usually refers to a person, and people do fly in planes.

(e) Do you know the time?

Ambiguity: This question involves a pragmatic ambiguity, rather than a structural one. The question could be a request for information (like "what time is it?"); in this case, an appropriate response would be "Four o'clock." It could also be a question about whether or not someone knows what time it is; in this case, an appropriate response would be "yes" or "no."

Likely: The question is a request for information about what time it is.

Knowledge: Asking someone if they know something is usually interpreted as a request for information.

(f) <u>Concerned with spreading racial violence, the president called</u>
<u>a press conference.</u>

Ambiguity: "Spreading" could be an adjective, in which case the president is concerned with racial violence which is spreading. Or, "spreading racial violence" could be a gerundive verb phrase whose unexpressed subject is "the president", in which case he is concerned because he is spreading racial violence.

Likely: "Spreading" is an adjective.

Knowledge: It is unlikely that a president would be responsible for spreading racial violence, and more unlikely that he or she would call a press conference in that event.

7. *Transition Network.*

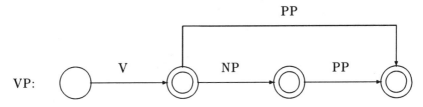

8. *Semantic Networks.*

A.   i. Birds fly.

FLY (BIRDS)

ii. The student understands the question.

UNDERSTANDS (THE STUDENT, THE QUESTION)

iii. Penguins do not fly.

NOT (FLY (PENGUINS))

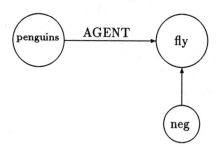

iv. The wind is in the willows.

IN (THE WIND, THE WILLOWS)

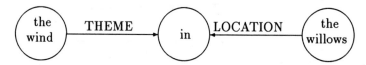

v. Kathy loves her cat.

LOVES (KATHY, (POSS (KATHY, CAT)))

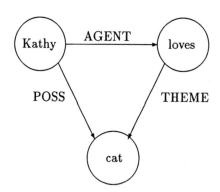

B.   i. *Seals swim swiftly.*

SWIFTLY (SWIM (SEALS))

ii. The student doesn't understand the question.

NOT (UNDERSTAND (THE STUDENT, THE QUESTION))

iii. The pen is on the table.

ON (THE PEN, THE TABLE)

iv. My dog eats bones.

EATS ((POSS (I, DOG)), BONES)

v. Emily gives money to charity.

GIVES (EMILY, MONEY, CHARITY)

ISBN 0-03-054984-1

9 780030 549847